simon sargon

a solo collection

Edited by J. Mark Dunn

volume II: shabbat

American composer and pianist SIMON SARGON was born in 1938 in Bombay, India, of Sephardic-Indian and Ashkenazic-Russian descent, and brought to the United States as an infant. He took private piano lessons with Mieczyslaw Horszowski, and studied music theory at Brandeis University, where he graduated magna cum laude. He went on to study composition at the Juilliard School under Vincent Persichetti, and at the Aspen School of Music under Darius Milhaud.

Sargon taught at Sarah Lawrence College from 1965-1968; and served as head of the voice department of the Rubin Academy of Music in Jerusalem from 1971-1974. In 1974 he was appointed Director of Music at Temple Emanu-El in Dallas, Texas, where he served until his retirement in September 2001. In 1984, he joined the music faculty of Southern Methodist University, where he currently serves as Professor of Composition.

Sargon's works are published by Transcontinental Music, Boosey and Hawkes, Southern Music and Lawson-Guild. He is listed in Baker's Biography and the International Who's Who in Music (eleventh edition). His work as both composer and pianist may be heard on the New World, Transcontinental Music Publications, Crystal, Ongaku and Gasparo labels. Mr. Sargon's works have also been recorded: Shema (available from Transcontinental Music), A Clear Midnight (GSCD 333), Renew Unto Us A Good Year (available from Transcontinental Music) and Flame of the Lord (GSCD 347).

HEBREW TRANSLITERATION PRONUNCIATION GUIDE

VOWELS

a = ah, as in father
ai = i, as in ice
e = eh, as in bed
ei = aye, as in plate
i = ee, as in see
o = oh, as in go
u = oo, as in food

CONSONANTS

ch as in German "Ach"-not ch as in "cheese"
g is hard
tz, as in boats, often begins a word

©2002 TRANSCONTINENTAL MUSIC PUBLICATIONS – NEW JEWISH MUSIC PRESS
A DIVISION OF THE UNION OF AMERICAN HEBREW CONGREGATIONS
633 THIRD AVENUE – NEW YORK, NY 10017 – 212.650.4101
FAX 212.650.4109 – www.TranscontinentalMusic.com – tmp@uahc.org

Printed in the United States of America
ISBN 0-8074-0824-7
Design by Joel N. Eglash
10 9 8 7 6 5 4 3 2 1

Simon Sargon
A Solo Collection Volume II

Table of Contents

for Rabbi Sheldon Zimmerman
Eicha Ashir

Rabbi Joseph Zvi Rimmon *(1899-1958)*

Simon A. Sargon

4

shir _____ al ha-rim ug-va - ot, _____ vei - lo - him hu t' - va -

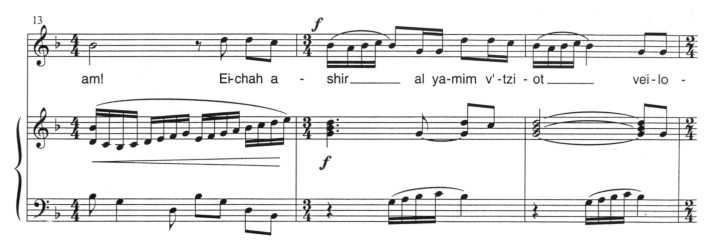

am! Ei-chah a - shir _____ al ya-mim v'-tzi - ot _____ vei - lo -

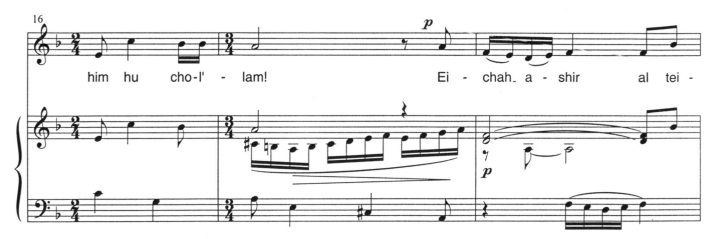

him hu cho-l'-lam! Ei - chah _ a - shir al tei -

veil _ um - lo - ah vei - lo - him _____ hu tzi - vah! A -

shir_____ l'-yo- tzeir __ ha - kol, l'-yo- tseir__ha-kol, v'-na- a-

le__ al ha-kol, lei - lo - him_____ a - shi - rah, lei - lo-

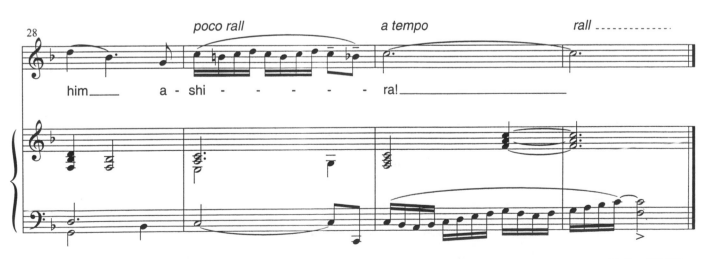

him____ a - shi - - - - ra!_____

Dallas, 7/8/98

6

V'sham'ru

Liturgy

Simon A. Sargon

Dallas, TX, 15 Jan 1982

For the 50th Wedding Anniversary of Jessonda and Albert Fox

Eloheinu, Velohei Avoteinu

Liturgy

Simon A. Sargon

Voice: E-lo-hei-nu vei-lo-hei___ a-vo-tei-nu, r'-tseih vi-m'-nu-cha-

tei-nu. Ka-d'-shei-nu b'-mitz-vo-te-cha v'-tein chel-kei-nu b'-to-ra-

te-cha. Sab'-ei-nu mi-tu-ve-cha v'-sa-m'-chei-nu bi-shu-a-

te - cha, v'-ta - heir____ li - bei - nu l'- ov-d'- cha____ b'- e -

piu mosso, forcefully

met. V'- han-chi - lei - nu,____ A - do-nai El - lo - hei - nu, b'- a - ha - vah ù - v'- ra-

sostenuto   *a tempo*

tzon Shab - bat, Shab - bat____ kod - she - cha,

10

v' - ya - nu - chu vah___ Yis - ra - eil, Yisra - eil m' - ka - d' -shei sh' -

me - cha. Ba - ruch A - tah___ A - do - nai, m' - ka - deish ha-Shab -

bat, m' - ka - deish ha-Shab - - bat.

Dallas, TX
June 1, 1989

To the memory of Henry X. Salzberger

R'tzeih

Liturgy

Simon A. Sargon

tzon ta - mid a - vo - dat Yis - ra - eil_____ a - me - cha._____ Sh' -

foch ru - cha cha, ru - cha - cha a - lei - nu, Sh' - foch ru - cha - cha a -

lei - nu,_____ v' - te - che - ze - nah ei - nei - nu b' - shu - v' - cha l' - Tzi -

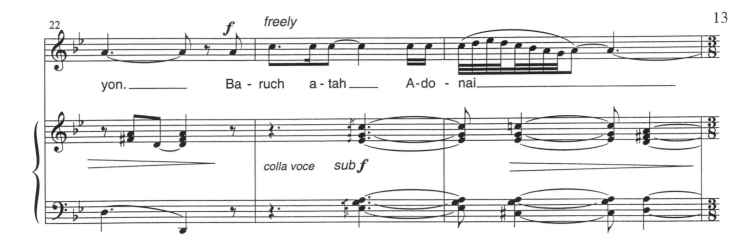

for the Bar-Mitzvah of David Zilbermann

Sim Shalom

Morning Liturgy

Simon A. Sargon

Sim sha-lom,___ to-vah___ uv-ra-chah, chein va-che-sed v'-ra-cha-mim, a-lei-nu, a-lei-nu v'-al kol Yis-ra-eil; a-lei-nu, a-lei-nu v'-

rat cha - yim___ v' - a - ha - vat___ che - sed, utz - da - kah___

uv - ra - chah v' - ra - cha - mim,___ v' - cha - - yim, v' -

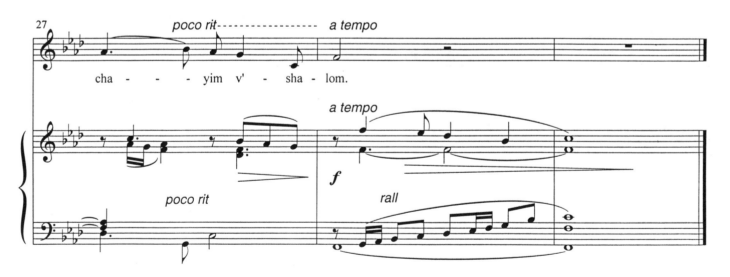

cha - - yim v' - sha - lom.

Commissioned by Karen and Reid Heller
in memory of Sindee Rosenaur

Shehashalom Shelo
(Song of Peace)

Liturgy

Simon A. Sargon

lo
lone.
ya - sim___ a - lei - nu_____ b'ra-chah v'- sha-
Oh grant us Your bles - sing._____ The bles - sing of

lom.
peace
Mis' - mol u - mi-ya - min
pro - found___ and___ true.
bra-chah v'- sha-
The bles - sing of

lom
peace.
al Yis-ra - eil,_____ b'ra-chah v'- sha - lom,
Grant un - to us._____ The bles - sing of peace.
al Yis-ra-
Grant un - to

eil_____ b'ra-chah v'- sha - lom.
us_____ the bles - sing of peace.
accel.
cresc -

lo
lone.
ya-sim___ a-lei___ nu___ b'ra-chah v'-sha-
Oh grant us Your bles - sing.___ The bles-sing of

lom,
peace,
b'ra-cha v'-sha- lom.___ Mis'-mol u-mi-ya-
the bles-sing of peace.___ Pro-found___ and___

min.
true.
Ha-ra-cha-man___ y'-va-reich et a-
Oh grant un - to us.___ All the bles-sings of

mo,
peace.
et a-mo___ va-sha-
Grant un - to us.___ The bles-sing of

Sha-lom___ she - lo,
For peace comes from God.
sha - lom___ she-
lom.
peace.

lo.___
bove.

Dec. 11, 1997

To the memory of Ruby Cohen Polmer

Oh Pray for the Peace of Jerusalem

Psalm 122: 6-9

Simon A. Sargon

24

breth-ren and com-pan-ions' sakes___ I will now say: Peace be with-in___ thee. For the

sake of the house of the Lord our God. I will seek thy good. Peace be wtih-

in thy walls. Peace___ in thee. ___

Dallas, May 1975

For Cantor Sarah J. Sager

Hamavdil

Havdalah

Simon A. Sargon

26

tov, sha - vu - a tov, sha - vu - a tov, sha - vu - a

tov, sha - vu - a tov, sha - vua - a tov. Sha - vu - a

tov sha - vu - a tov sha - vu - a tov.

Dallas, TX
Feb. 4, 1991

To the memory of Ann Salfield

Nachamu, Ami

Isaiah 40:1,2

Simon A. Sargon

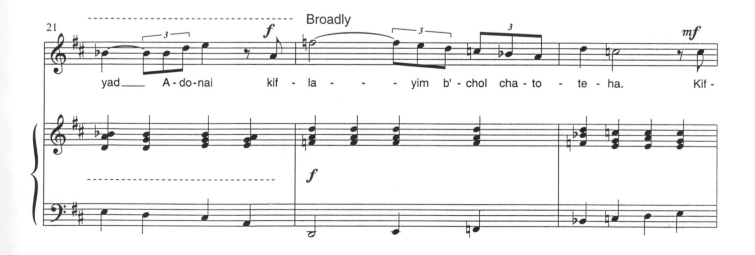

la - yim b'-chol cha-to-te-ha; kif-la-yim, kif-la-yim___ b'-chol cha-to -

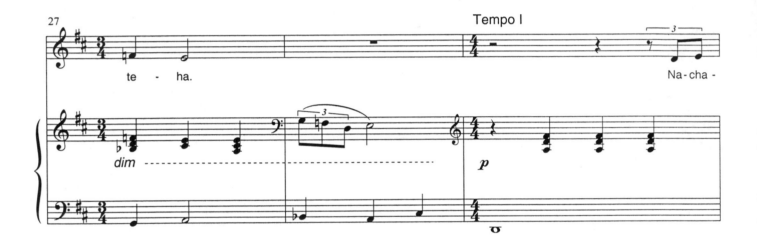

te - ha. Na-cha-

mu, na-cha-mu a-mi yo-mar E-lo-hei-chem; na-cha-mu, na-cha-mu a-mi

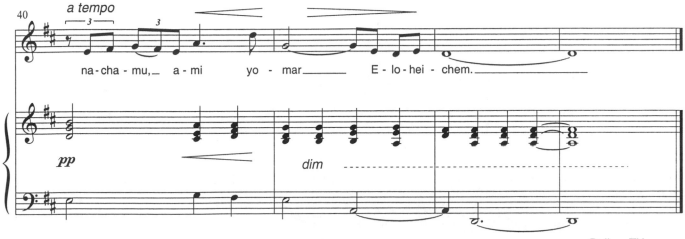

Dallas, TX
5/26/96

EICHA ASHIR

How can I sing of mountains and hills,
when it is God who planted them?

How can I sing of seas and deserts,
when it is God who begot them?

And how can I sing of earth and its fullness,
when it is God who bade them be?

I shall sing to God who fashioned all and is beyond all -
it is to God I shall sing!

אֵיכָה אָשִׁיר עֲל־הָרִים וּגְבָעוֹת
וֵאלֹהִים הוּא טְבָעָם!

אֵיכָה אָשִׁיר עֲל־יַמִּים וְצִיּוֹת
וֵאלֹהִים הוּא חוֹלְלָם!

אֵיכָה אָשִׁיר עֲל־תֵבֵל וּמְלוֹאָהּ
וֵאלֹהִים הוּא צִוָּהּ!

אָשִׁיר לְיוֹצֵר הַכֹּל וְנֶעֱלָה עֲל־כֹּל
לֵאלֹהִים אָשִׁירָה!

V'SHAM'RU

The people of Israel shall keep the Sabbath, observing the Sabbath in every generation as
a covenant for all time. It is a sign forever between Me and the people of Israel, for in six
days the Eternal God made heaven and earth, and on the seventh day God rested from
God's labors.

וְשָׁמְרוּ בְנֵי־יִשְׂרָאֵל אֶת־הַשַּׁבָּת,
לַעֲשׂוֹת אֶת־הַשַּׁבָּת לְדֹרֹתָם
בְּרִית עוֹלָם. בֵּינִי וּבֵין בְּנֵי
יִשְׂרָאֵל אוֹת הִיא לְעֹלָם, כִּי
שֵׁשֶׁת יָמִים עָשָׂה יְיָ אֶת־הַשָּׁמַיִם
וְאֶת־הָאָרֶץ, וּבַיּוֹם הַשְּׁבִיעִי
שָׁבַת וַיִּנָּפַשׁ.

ELOHEINU, VELOHEI AVOTEINU

Our God and God of ages past, may our rest on this day be
pleasing in Your sight. Sanctify us with Your Mitzvot, and
let Your Torah be our way of life. Satisfy us with Your
goodness, gladden us with Your salvation, and purify our
hearts to serve You in truth. In Your gracious love, Adonai
our God, let Your holy Sabbath remain our heritage, that all
Israel, hallowing Your name, may find rest and peace.
Blessed is God, for the Sabbath and its holiness.

אֱלֹהֵינוּ וֵאלֹהֵי אֲבוֹתֵינוּ, רְצֵה בִמְנוּחָתֵנוּ. קַדְּשֵׁנוּ בְּמִצְוֹתֶיךָ
וְתֵן חֶלְקֵנוּ בְּתוֹרָתֶךָ. שַׂבְּעֵנוּ מִטּוּבֶךָ, וְשַׂמְּחֵנוּ בִּישׁוּעָתֶךָ,
וְטַהֵר לִבֵּנוּ לְעָבְדְּךָ בֶּאֱמֶת. וְהַנְחִילֵנוּ, יְיָ אֱלֹהֵינוּ, בְּאַהֲבָה
וּבְרָצוֹן שַׁבַּת קָדְשֶׁךָ, וְיָנוּחוּ בָהּ יִשְׂרָאֵל מְקַדְּשֵׁי שְׁמֶךָ. בָּרוּךְ
אַתָּה, יְיָ, מְקַדֵּשׁ הַשַּׁבָּת.

R'TZEIH

Adonai our God, may we, Your people Israel, be worthy in
our deeds and our prayer. Wherever we live, wherever we
seek You - in the land, in Zion, in all lands - You are our
God, whom alone we serve in reverence.

רְצֵה, יְיָ אֱלֹהֵינוּ, בְּעַמְּךָ יִשְׂרָאֵל, וּתְפִלָּתָם בְּאַהֲבָה תְקַבֵּל,
וּתְהִי לְרָצוֹן תָּמִיד עֲבוֹדַת יִשְׂרָאֵל עַמֶּךָ. שְׁפוֹךְ רוּחֲךָ עָלֵינוּ,
וְתֶחֱזֶינָה עֵינֵינוּ בְּשׁוּבְךָ לְצִיּוֹן בָּרוּךְ אַתָּה, יְיָ,
שֶׁאוֹתְךָ לְבַדְּךָ בְּיִרְאָה נַעֲבוֹד.

SIM SHALOM

Peace, happiness, and blessing; grace and love and mercy;
may these descend on us, on all Israel, and all the world.

שִׂים שָׁלוֹם, טוֹבָה וּבְרָכָה, חֵן וָחֶסֶד וְרַחֲמִים, עָלֵינוּ וְעַל־
כָּל־יִשְׂרָאֵל עַמֶּךָ.

Bless us, our Creator, one and all, with the light of Your
presence; for by that light, O God, You have revealed to us
the law of life: to love kindness and justice and mercy, to
seek blessing, life, and peace.

בָּרְכֵנוּ אָבִינוּ, כֻּלָּנוּ כְּאֶחָד, בְּאוֹר פָּנֶיךָ, כִּי בְאוֹר פָּנֶיךָ נָתַתָּ
לָּנוּ, יְיָ אֱלֹהֵינוּ, תּוֹרַת חַיִּים, וְאַהֲבַת חֶסֶד, וּצְדָקָה וּבְרָכָה
וְרַחֲמִים, וְחַיִּים וְשָׁלוֹם.

SHEHASHALOM SHELO

May the God of peace help us find blessing and peace for all, far and near. May God in mercy bless God's people with peace.

Then we will live to see our children and their children busy with Torah and Mitzvot, and all Israel at peace. Blessed is the mighty God, the eternal Creator, the Author of peace.

שֶׁהַשָּׁלוֹם שֶׁלּוֹ יָשִׂים עָלֵינוּ בְּרָכָה וְשָׁלוֹם. מִשְּׂמֹאל וּמִיָּמִין, עַל יִשְׂרָאֵל שָׁלוֹם. הָרַחֲמָן הוּא יְבָרֵךְ אֶת עַמּוֹ בַשָּׁלוֹם.

וְנִזְכּוּ לִרְאוֹת בָּנִים וּבְנֵי בָנִים עוֹסְקִים בַּתּוֹרָה וּבְמִצְוֹת, עַל יִשְׂרָאֵל שָׁלוֹם. פֶּלֶא יוֹעֵץ, אֵל גִּבּוֹר, אֲבִי עַד, שַׂר שָׁלוֹם.

HAMAVDIL

You teach us to distinguish between the commonplace and the holy: teach us also to transform our sins to merits. Let those who love you be numerous as the sands and the stars.

Day has declined, the shadows are gone; we call to the One whose word is good. The sentry says: 'Morning will come, though the night seems long.'

Your righteousness is a majestic mountain: forgive our sins. Let them be as yesterday when it is past, as a watch in the night.

A good week...

הַמַּבְדִּיל בֵּין קֹדֶשׁ לְחוֹל,
חַטֹּאתֵינוּ הוּא יִמְחַל,
זַרְעֵנוּ וְכַסְפֵּנוּ יַרְבֶּה כַּחוֹל,
וְכַכּוֹכָבִים בַּלָּיְלָה.

שָׁבוּעַ טוֹב . . .

יוֹם פָּנָה כְּצֵל תֹּמֶר,
אֶקְרָא לָאֵל, עָלַי גֹּמֵר;
אָמַר שׁוֹמֵר, אָתָא בֹקֶר,
וְגַם־לָיְלָה.

שָׁבוּעַ טוֹב . . .

צִדְקָתְךָ כְּהַר תָּבוֹר,
עַל חֲטָאַי עָבוֹר תַּעֲבוֹר,
כְּיוֹם אֶתְמוֹל כִּי יַעֲבוֹר,
וְאַשְׁמוּרָה בַלָּיְלָה.

שָׁבוּעַ טוֹב . . .

NACHAMU, AMI

Comfort, oh comfort My people, says your God.
Speak tenderly to Jerusalem, and declare to her
That her term of service is over, that her iniquity is expiated;
For she has received at the hand of God double for all her sins.

נַחֲמוּ נַחֲמוּ עַמִּי יֹאמַר אֱלֹהֵיכֶם:
דַּבְּרוּ עַל־לֵב יְרוּשָׁלַםִ וְקִרְאוּ אֵלֶיהָ
כִּי מָלְאָה צְבָאָהּ כִּי נִרְצָה עֲוֹנָהּ
כִּי לָקְחָה מִיַּד יְהוָה כִּפְלַיִם בְּכָל־חַטֹּאתֶיהָ: